THOMAS JEFFERSON
Grows a Nation

BY PEGGY THOMAS   ILLUSTRATIONS BY STACY INNERST

CALKINS CREEK

AN IMPRINT OF HIGHLIGHTS

Honesdale, Pennsylvania

Monticello

To Kent L. Brown Jr., for encouraging writers to grow
—PT

For my grandfather A. D. Cook, physician and farmer
—SI

Acknowledgments
I would like to thank the enthusiastic guides at Monticello, Thomas Jefferson's home,
for helping me as I walked in Thomas's footsteps. The staff at the Massachusetts Historical Society
answered all my questions about Jefferson's *Notes on the State of Virginia*,
and Kevin Daugherty, education director of the Illinois Agriculture in the Classroom program,
Bloomington, offered much encouragement, which was greatly appreciated.
Special thanks to Anna Berkes, research librarian at the Jefferson Library,
for guiding my research and sharing her insights;
my editor Carolyn P. Yoder;
and Fran Thomas for being an exceptional research assistant.
—PT

NO OCCUPATION is so Delightful TO ME AS THE CULTURE of the EARTH

Thomas Jefferson loved to grow things.
At Monticello, his home in Virginia, he grew potatoes, peppers, pippins, peaches, juniper, larkspur, and peas. Flowers hugged his house, fruit trees dotted the orchard, and wheat marched down the mountainside. And throughout his lifetime, he scattered seeds, like a brisk wind, around the world.

After planting the seed of freedom writing the Declaration
of Independence, Thomas had something new to nurture.
And like any farmer imagining the harvest of a newly tilled field,
Thomas envisioned a nation of farmers.
But one weed threatened Thomas's vision.

"Cultivators of the earth are the most valuable citizens. They are the most vigorous, the most independant, the most virtuous, and they are tied to their country and wedded to it's liberty and interests by the most lasting bands."

For years, famous French naturalist Count Buffon had been belittling America. The wildlife was inferior, he said, "Shrivelled." "Diminished." Sheep were "meagre, and their flesh less juicy." A jaguar was no bigger than a beagle, and dogs were "mute." The New World, he argued, had nothing as grand as an elephant, and the weather produced an infestation of lowly reptiles and insects.

If readers believed Buffon's lies, who would trade with the states or travel across the Atlantic to become a new citizen? So Thomas did what he did best.

He pulled out his pen, uprooted every mistake in Buffon's books, and planted the truth in his own book called *Notes on the State of Virginia*. "The skeleton of the mammoth . . . bespeaks an animal of five or six times" the size of an elephant, he said. And relying on scientific evidence, he showed that one South American tapir weighed more than Buffon's entire list of animals unique to Europe. Thomas also boasted about American mountains, especially his view of the Blue Ridge range. "This scene is worth a voyage across the Atlantic."

Figure 1

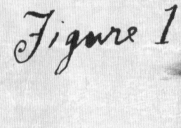

Figure 2

In July 1784, Thomas took his own voyage. The United States Congress appointed him minister plenipotentiary to France. Now, Thomas could confront Buffon personally. He even purchased a panther skin he spied on the way to the ship. "I bought it for half a Jo," he said, "determining to carry it to France to convince Monsieur Buffon of his mistake."

Over dinner, Thomas and Buffon spoke of panthers, cougars, and elk. "I told him also that the reindeer could walk under the belly of our moose," said Thomas. But Buffon was not convinced.

Thomas rode away from Count Buffon's house more determined than ever to prove that America was just as great and strong as Europe. If Buffon could see a real moose, the largest and most magnificent animal, surely he would never belittle the United States again. Thomas wrote to friends and pleaded, "The skin, the skeleton and the horns . . . would be an acquisition here more precious than you could conceive."

It took months, but on June 16, 1787, Thomas opened a letter from the governor of New Hampshire. A moose was on its way. Another letter described how, that winter, a team of twenty soldiers "sallied forth . . . and with Difficulty killed one in Vermont." It took two weeks to cut a road through the snow to haul the carcass by sleigh to the governor's home, where "Every Engine was set at work to preserve the Bones and . . . the skins" just as Thomas had instructed.

The summer passed. No moose arrived. Even with the usual long intervals between trans-Atlantic communications, Thomas thought he would have heard news. By September, Thomas assumed the moose was lost for good. Then, in a flurry of delayed letters, he learned that back in May the moose had been left on the docks in Portsmouth, New Hampshire, and had to be carted to Boston and loaded on a ship to France.

On October 1, nine months after the moose hunt, a large crate arrived on Thomas's doorstep. From the smell, he could probably tell what it was. Eagerly he opened it and laid the contents on the floor, to the disgust of his guests. A femur, a hoof, bits of fur, and antlers as wide as his arms. Without delay, Thomas sent the massive yet raggedy all-American moose to Buffon.

Years later, Thomas recalled how Buffon, upon seeing the monumental moose, finally changed his mind. Unfortunately, Buffon died without ever revising his books. Thomas's *Notes*, however, inspired many writers, including Washington Irving, Henry David Thoreau, and Ralph Waldo Emerson, to promote America as a big, beautiful, and bountiful nation.

Thomas's job as minister to France was to grow America's economy. Before the Revolutionary War, Americans had to rely on Great Britain to sell their products. Now the United States had to cultivate its own commerce, and Thomas was perfect for the job. He established trade agreements to help New Englanders sell whale oil and Southerners sell tobacco. But, Thomas noticed, many Europeans knew little about what his country had to offer.

Soon, Thomas was patriotically passing out persimmon plants and pecans. He scattered sumac seeds among his friends, as well as sweet gum, sassafras, and sorrel. In Thomas's garden on the corner of Rue de Berri and the Champs-Élysées, Cherokee corn stalks waved over swelling watermelons and cantaloupes.

While Thomas tutored the French in American produce,
he harnessed his curiosity to benefit farmers back home. On trips
through France and Italy, Thomas sketched windmills and
wheelbarrows, visited vineyards and villages. He measured
mules in Marseille, cheese in Rozzano, and bricks in Bordeaux.

*"Every discovery which multiplies the subsistence of men,
must be a matter of joy to every friend to humanity."*

Wandering among market stalls looking for new and better crops, Thomas noticed that the French preferred dry rice. But U.S. farmers grew "swamp" rice and often suffered from mosquitoes and malaria. If they switched to dry rice, Southern growers would be healthier and wealthier.

"The greatest service which can be rendered any country is, to add an useful plant to its culture."

Thomas began searching for the right kind. He asked ship captains for rice from far-off lands and appealed to the child prince of Cochin China where, it was said, the whitest rice grew.

On April 13, 1787, Thomas celebrated his forty-fourth birthday riding a mule over the Alps to find the highly prized dry rice of Italy. It was illegal to export grain without permission, so Thomas stuffed his pockets full. Risking the death penalty, he smuggled it out.

Back in Paris, Thomas shipped sacks of rice to farmers in South Carolina and Georgia. Although the dry rice helped family farmers, it failed as a cash crop. But Thomas was not discouraged.

Olive trees! he said, "should be the object of the Carolina patriot." Soon, hundreds of olive saplings set sail for America, where he hoped olive oil would "be the source of the greatest wealth and happiness."

It wasn't. The climate was wrong and the plants died. But Thomas remained optimistic.

"I have always thought that if in the experiments to introduce ... new plants, one species in an hundred is found useful and succeeds, the ninety nine found otherwise are more than paid for."

In 1789, Thomas also set sail for America and soon became secretary of state for President George Washington. New York City, the nation's capital, was a hothouse of dispute. The once united Founding Fathers were growing apart. Treasury secretary Alexander Hamilton's vision of a nation of cities and factories tangled with Thomas's vision of small towns and family farms.

To escape the noise, Thomas joined James Madison and rode north to let the greenery calm his constant headaches. As Thomas trotted beneath the sheltering arms of maple trees, he was convinced that maple sugar would keep farmers from running off to manufacturing jobs. It "promises us an abundant supply of sugar at home," he said. "What a blessing" to replace sugarcane grown by slaves in the West Indies and sold at a steep price by Great Britain.

Thomas led the experiment by planting a sugar orchard at Monticello.

The experiment failed and maple syrup never flowed across the nation as Thomas envisioned. The trees needed the cold winters of the North to produce sap.

But Thomas was plagued by another concern. The United States had been invaded.

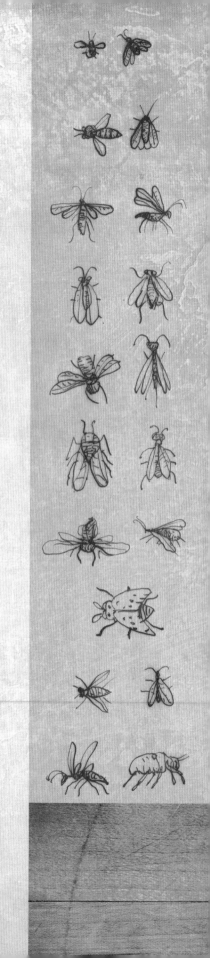

Farmers named the invader the Hessian fly. It had devoured wheat fields on Long Island and turned south to chew through New Jersey, leaving nothing more than shriveled stalks in its wake. The pest was so destructive that England, afraid the fly would hitch a ride and eat its way across Europe, banned American shipments of the grain.

Thomas set up a committee to study "the best means of preventing or destroying the Insect," and on his trip north he quizzed farmers about the fly's habits. What time in the season did the fly appear? What part of the plant did it eat? How long was it in *"Worm-State"*?

On his desk in Philadelphia, the nation's new capital, Thomas witnessed flies hatching from their chrysalises, examined their bodies under a microscope, and watched as a female, "between the size of a gnat & musketoe," laid its eggs.

Thomas advised farmers to plant late, manure well, and burn the stubble after harvest. But still the fly moved south. And so did Thomas.

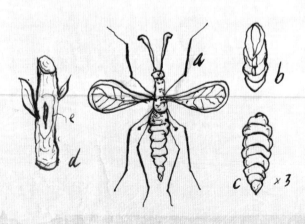

In 1794, Thomas left Philadelphia, eager to live at Monticello again. But overgrown fences and weedy fields greeted him. "A 10. years abandonment of them . . . to the unprincipled ravages of overseers, has brought on a degree of degradation far beyond what I had expected." Thomas plowed ahead. "I return to farming with an ardour which I scarcely knew in my youth," he wrote. "Instead of writing 10. or 12. letters a day, which I have been in the habit of doing . . . I put off answering my letters now, farmer-like, till a rainy day."

Builders knocked down walls to enlarge his house while Thomas inspected his fields. He hoped that all the changes he made would be "more productive . . . and perhaps [be] of some utility to my neighbors." While others still grew one crop year after year and plowed in straight lines over hills and valleys, Thomas rotated his crops to nurture the soil, plowed along the contours of the mountain to catch the rainfall, and fertilized with cartloads of manure.

"The plough is to the farmer,
what the wand is to the Sorcerer."

Fig. A

Thomas also had time to tinker. He built the new plow device he had described in his travel journal from France. Called "the mould-board of least resistance," it was a wedge that cut into the earth, lifted the clod, and turned it over with ease.

Thomas's mathematical precision also assured "that it may be made by the most bungling carpenter." Thomas shared his design with other farmers and sent a model to the British Board of Agriculture and the French Society of Agriculture, which later awarded him a gold medal for his achievements.

While his moldboard churned up the soil at home, disputes between the Federalists and Republicans churned up the capital.

Thomas returned to politics, and after serving as John Adams's vice president, he became the third president of the United States in 1801. With an unfinished White House and the rutted roads of Washington, D.C., Thomas felt right at home. Dressed in his usual farmer attire, he spent each morning meeting with cabinet members and writing letters. In the afternoon, Thomas didn't even have to change his clothes before jumping onto a horse to ride through the countryside and collect plants.

Thomas didn't have a garden at the White House, but he visited the open-air markets that he established in the city. He shared seeds with the farmers and recorded when new vegetables were harvested. He even ordered poplar trees to plant along Pennsylvania Avenue.

Through the geraniums growing on the windowsill, Thomas could watch cattle graze in the distant meadow. How many times did his imagination look even farther west across an entire continent to picture "a rising nation, spread over a wide and fruitful land"?

The United States could never expand as Thomas envisioned while other nations controlled territory west of the Mississippi River. In the fall of 1802, France closed its port of New Orleans, leaving U.S. flatboats filled with tobacco, cotton, furs, feathers, beef, bacon, and beans stranded along the Mississippi River. That was nearly half of what America produced.

To free up the port and prevent France from establishing a colony in the West, Thomas sought a peaceful solution by sending James Monroe to France to negotiate the purchase of New Orleans.

To Thomas's surprise, France offered to sell the entire Louisiana Territory. Could a president purchase land on behalf of a nation? No one was sure. Some said it was not in his power. Others complained it was a waste of money.

But Thomas's bold action reaped a country twice its original size. For fifteen million dollars, the United States grew more than eight hundred thousand square miles in one day. Now it reached to the Rocky Mountains, stretched north to Canada, and dipped its toe in the Gulf of Mexico.

It also guaranteed Thomas's vision. "The fertility of the country, its climate and extent, promise . . . a wide-spread field for the blessings of freedom and equal laws."

Louisiana Territory

For years, Thomas had yearned to discover what lay in the vast wilderness to the west. What was the soil like? What plants grew there? Did the mammoth still exist? Soon, he and the entire nation would learn the answers.

Thomas had been organizing an expedition led by his private secretary, Meriwether Lewis, to "explore the Missouri river, & . . . the most direct & practicable water communication across this continent." Lewis and his partner, William Clark, prepared to travel over foreign land. But now with the Louisiana Territory, the explorers would ford *American* streams and climb *American* mountains.

With each shipment Lewis and Clark sent back, the knowledge of the country blossomed. Thomas pored over each report and displayed skins of antelope, deer, prairie dog, and fox. Boxes of seeds arrived: snowberries, Pani corn, currants, peas, and beans. Soon, farms in the East were fenced with prickly Osage orange, and fashionable gardens featured Oregon grape holly.

In 1809, after two terms in office, Thomas retired. Finally, he could improve his home at Monticello, just as he improved his country. "I am constantly in my garden or farm," he wrote, "as exclusively employed out of doors as I was within doors when at Washington, and I find myself infinitely happier in my new mode of life." Always humming, Thomas inspected his farm fields and followed his grandchildren as they ran ahead to check for new blooms in the flower garden.

He continued to send seeds to friends, but now he could test his own in his one-thousand-foot-long kitchen garden—lettuce from France, dry rice from Italy, gooseberries from the banks of the Missouri, and corn from the Mandan Indians—all fruits of his labor as minister to France, secretary of state, vice president, and president.

Thomas had watched a nation sprout and grow, and only one thing remained to be done—prepare the soil for the future.

"*The field of knolege is the common property of all mankind.*"

In a worn-out field six miles northwest of Monticello, Thomas measured out the foundation for the University of Virginia and struck the first peg into the ground in 1817. Later, he wrote, "I am closing the last scenes of life by fashioning and fostering an establishment for the instruction of those who are to come after us."

For the next eight years, Thomas plotted out classrooms and dormitories, made a list of plants for the school's botanical garden, and watched his "academical village" grow.

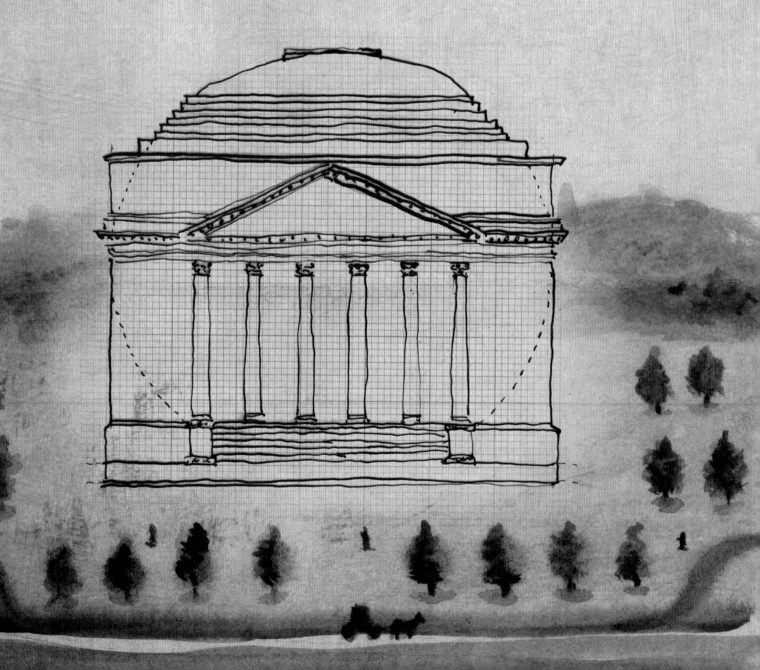

On July 4, 1826, at the age of eighty-three, Thomas Jefferson died. It was the fiftieth anniversary of the Declaration of Independence, nearly forty years since he had smuggled fistfuls of rice, and twenty-three years from the moment he celebrated that the United States had grown twice its size.

Thomas loved to grow things. He grew seeds and science, liberty and learning, farmers, freedom, and democracy.

"Planting a new world with the seeds of just government, will produce a remarkable aera in the history of mankind."

·SEEDS·

THOMAS TODAY

Thomas once wrote: "When I first entered on the stage of public life . . . I came to a resolution never . . . to wear any other character than that of a farmer." He meant that he would always be sensible, honest, and plainspoken, attributes he admired in people who, like him, made their living off the land. Thomas loved seeds and soil and pondered ways to improve agriculture, but he rarely dug in the earth. At Monticello, hundreds of slaves plowed, weeded, pruned, and harvested. In the 1700s, owning slaves was common among Southern landowners, including Thomas. But today it is difficult to understand how the writer of the Declaration of Independence could own slaves. How could he treat another man as property and still write the phrase "all men are created equal"? Thomas proposed the first laws against the importation of slaves and supported the ban of slavery in the Northwest Territories, yet over his lifetime he owned six hundred people.

We must decide for ourselves how slavery taints the legacy of Thomas Jefferson. Fortunately, his words spoke louder than his actions. Slavery was finally abolished in 1865, yet Thomas's inspirational writings live on and continue to affect the way we live today. From "all men are created equal" grew the civil rights movement and the women's rights movement, and it will remain the kernel of hope for those who struggle for equality in the future.

One struggle the Founding Fathers faced was defining the United States. The Republicans saw a nation based on agriculture and farmers, while Federalists envisioned a country of merchants and industry. Eventually this split became the two parties that dominate our modern democratic system. Thomas wasn't entirely against commerce. "They admit me a friend to agriculture," he said, "and suppose me an enemy to the only means of disposing of it's produce." However, Thomas did all he could to promote his ideal—encouraging the use of different crops and spreading the news of agricultural innovations.

He succeeded in several ways. Many of the rare and novel plants that Thomas experimented with in his garden are now common products on grocery store shelves: tomatoes, peppers, eggplant, okra, sesame oil, kale, chickpeas, and cayenne pepper. American farmers continue to feed the nation and produce more each

JEFFERSONIA DIPHYLLA

On May 18, 1792, botanist Benjamin Smith Barton announced that he had named a wildflower after Thomas. Barton said of Thomas that, "in botany and in zoology, the information of this gentleman is equalled by that of few persons in the United-States." The plant, more commonly called twinleaf, lives in shady, moist woodlands from Canada to Georgia and as far west as Indiana.

year for export to other nations; and with better technology, they can produce more on less land.

Thomas did much more nurturing than I could squeeze into this book, and as all gardeners know, not every seed germinates. At least not right away. His "Scheme for a System of Agricultural Societies," which he wrote in 1811, did not bear fruit until years later when the United States Department of Agriculture was founded. Olive trees that failed to grow in South Carolina now thrive in commercial groves in California.

Thomas never seemed to let failure stop him. He always had another project to work on and more information to share. That resilience and optimism are important parts of the American spirit, and his sense of order is imprinted on the landscape. In 1785, the Continental Congress enacted Thomas's plan for selling land west of the original thirteen colonies. Surveyors divided land into 36 square miles called townships, which were subdivided into 160-acre parcels (the amount of land a farmer needed to make a living). If you fly across the country, you can still see Thomas's neat jigsaw of green, brown, and gold squares and the "extensive and fertile Country" he helped cultivate.

—PT

Th: Jefferson
1743–1826

TIMELINE

1743	Thomas is born on April 13.
1775–76	Member of Continental Congress.
1776	Drafts the Declaration of Independence.
1779–81	Governor of Virginia.
1784–89	Commissioner and minister to France.
1787	Publishes *Notes on the State of Virginia*.
1790–93	U.S. secretary of state for George Washington.
1794	Retires to Monticello.
1797–1801	Vice president under John Adams.
1801–09	U.S. president.
1803	Louisiana Purchase concludes. Lewis and Clark Expedition begins.
1809	Retires to Monticello.
1817	Surveys land for the University of Virginia.
1826	Thomas dies on July 4 at Monticello.

LEARN MORE

SELECTED BIBLIOGRAPHY*

Betts, Edwin Morris, ed. *Thomas Jefferson's Garden Book, 1766–1824: With Relevant Extracts from His Other Writings*. Charlottesville, VA: Thomas Jefferson Memorial Foundation, 1999.

Buffon, George Louis Leclerc. *Buffon's Natural History: Containing a Theory of the Earth, a General History of Man, of the Brute Creation, and of Vegetables, Minerals, &. &*. From the French, with notes by the translator. Vol. 7. London: H. D. Symonds, 1807.

Dugatkin, Lee Alan. *Mr. Jefferson and the Giant Moose: Natural History in Early America*. Chicago: University of Chicago Press, 2009.

Jefferson, Thomas. *Notes on the State of Virginia*. Coolidge Collection of Thomas Jefferson Manuscripts, Massachusetts Historical Society. masshist.org/thomasjeffersonpapers/index.php.

———. *The Papers of Thomas Jefferson*. Vols. 1, 4, and 8–33. Princeton, NJ: Princeton University Press, 1951 and 1953–2006.

———. Papers of Thomas Jefferson. Founders Early Access, Documents July 1804–March 3, 1809. University of Virginia Press, 2009. rotunda.upress.virginia.edu/founders/default.xqy?keys=FOEA-print-04-01-02-5793.

———. *The Papers of Thomas Jefferson*. Retirement Series, vols.1, 4, and 6. Princeton, NJ: Princeton University Press, 2004, 2007, and 2009.

———. "Scheme for a System of Agricultural Societies." In *Writings of Thomas Jefferson*. Edited by H. A. Washington. Vol. 9. Washington, DC: Taylor & Maury, 1854.

———. The Thomas Jefferson Papers. Series 1, General Correspondence, 1651–1827. Library of Congress, American Memory. memory.loc.gov/ammem/collections/jefferson_papers.

———. *The Works of Thomas Jefferson*. Federal ed., vol. 12. Edited by Paul Leicester Ford. New York: G. P. Putnam's Sons, 1904–1905.

———. *Writings: Autobiography, Notes on the State of Virginia, Public and Private Papers, Addresses, Letters*. New York: Library of America, 1984.

———. *The Writings of Thomas Jefferson*. Edited by Andrew A. Lipscomb and Albert E. Bergh. Vol. 14. Washington, DC: Thomas Jefferson Memorial Association of the United States, 1904.

Lewis, James E., Jr. *The Louisiana Purchase: Jefferson's Noble Bargain?* Monticello Monograph Series. Charlottesville, VA: Thomas Jefferson Foundation, 2003.

Meacham, Jon. *Thomas Jefferson: The Art of Power*. New York: Random House, 2012.

Thomas Jefferson Papers, 1743–1826. American Antiquarian Society.

Thomson, Keith. *Jefferson's Shadow: The Story of His Science*. New Haven, CT: Yale University Press, 2012.

Washington, George. *The Papers of George Washington*. Presidential Series, vol. 16, May 1–September 30, 1794. Edited by David R. Hoth and Carol S. Ebel. Charlottesville: University of Virginia Press, 2011.

Webster, Daniel. *The Private Correspondence of Daniel Webster*. Edited by Fletcher Webster. Boston: Little, Brown, 1857.

Wulf, Andrea. *Founding Gardeners: The Revolutionary Generation, Nature, and the Shaping of the American Nation*. New York: Alfred A. Knopf, 2012.

WEBSITES*
Discovering Lewis & Clark. lewis-clark.org
Monticello. monticello.org

TAKE A TRIP

The best way to learn about Thomas as a farmer is to walk the straight and orderly rows in his garden at Monticello. Smell the lavender, taste a freshly hulled pea, and see his vision of the United States rooted in the soil—a mix of all-American plants and vegetables from around the world. See a replica of his moldboard and take home heirloom seeds to plant in your own garden. Monticello is located outside of Charlottesville, Virginia, at 931 Thomas Jefferson Parkway, Charlottesville, Virginia 22902.

SOURCE NOTES*

The source of each quotation in this book is found below. The citation indicates the first words of the quotation and its document source. The sources are listed in the bibliography.

"No occupation is so delightful . . .": letter from Jefferson to Charles Willson Peale, August 20, 1811, *The Papers of Thomas Jefferson*, Retirement Series, vol. 4, pp. 93–94. Founders Online, National Archives, founders.archives.gov/documents/Jefferson/03-04-02-0090.

"Cultivators of the earth . . .": letter from Jefferson to John Jay, August 23, 1785, *The Papers of Thomas Jefferson*, vol. 8, pp. 426–428. Founders Online, National Archives, founders.archives.gov/documents/Jefferson/01-08-02-0333.

"Shrivelled." and "Diminished.": Buffon, p. 38. Open Library, archive.org/stream//buffonsnaturalhi07buff#page/38/mode/2up.

"meagre, and their flesh . . .": Ibid., p. 13. Open Library, archive.org/stream//buffonsnaturalhi07buff#page/13/mode/1up.

"mute.": Ibid., p. 18. Open Library, archive.org/stream//buffonsnaturalhi07buff#page/18/mode/1up.

"The skeleton of the mammoth . . .": Jefferson, "Notes on the State of Virginia," in *Writings*, p. 167.

"This scene is worth . . .": Ibid., p. 143.

"I bought it for . . .": Jefferson, in Webster, p. 371. Google books, books.google.com/books?id=lmwFAAAAQAAJ&q=moose#v=onepage&q=moose&f=true.

"I told him also . . .": Ibid., p. 372.

"The skin, the skeleton . . .": letter from Jefferson to William Whipple, January 7, 1786, *The Papers of Thomas Jefferson*, vol. 9, pp. 161–162. Founders Online, National Archives, founders.archives.gov/documents/Jefferson/01-09-02-0147.

"sallied forth . . .": letter from Jefferson to John Sullivan, April 16, 1787, *The Papers of Thomas Jefferson*, vol. 11, pp. 295–297. Founders Online, National Archives, founders.archives.gov/documents/Jefferson/01-11-02-0285.

"Every Engine was set . . .": Ibid.

"Every discovery which . . .": letter from Jefferson to Jeudy de l'Hommande, August 9, 1787, *The Papers of Thomas Jefferson*, vol. 12, p. 11. Founders Online, National Archives, founders.archives.gov/documents/Jefferson/01-12-02-0017.

"The greatest service . . .": Jefferson, "A Memorandum (Services to My Country)," in *Writings*, p. 703.

"should be the object . . .": letter from Jefferson to Ralph Izard, September 18, 1789, *The Papers of Thomas Jefferson*, vol. 15, pp. 443–445. Founders Online, National Archives, founders.archives.gov/documents/Jefferson/01-15-02-0435.

"be the source of . . .": letter from Jefferson to Edward Rutledge, September 18, 1789, *The Papers of Thomas Jefferson*, vol. 15, pp. 451–453. Founders Online, National Archives, founders.archives.gov/documents/Jefferson/01-15-02-0443.

"I have always thought . . .": letter from Jefferson to Samuel Vaughan, Jr., November 27, 1790, *The Papers of Thomas Jefferson*, vol. 18, pp. 97–98. Founders Online, National Archives, founders.archives.gov/documents/Jefferson/01-18-02-0068.

"promises us an abundant . . .": letter from Jefferson to William Drayton, May 1, 1791, *The Papers of Thomas Jefferson*, vol. 20, pp. 332–333. Founders Online, National Archives, founders.archives.gov/documents/Jefferson/01-20-02-0090.

"What a blessing": letter from Jefferson to Benjamin Vaughan, June 27, 1790, *The Papers of Thomas Jefferson*, vol. 16, pp. 578–580. Founders Online, National Archives, founders.archives.gov/documents/Jefferson/01-16-02-0342.

"the best means of preventing . . .": "American Philosophical Society's Circular on the Hessian Fly," April 17, 1792, *The Papers of Thomas Jefferson*, vol. 23, pp. 430–433. Founders Online, National Archives, founders.archives.gov/documents/Jefferson/01-23-02-0384.

"*Worm-State*": Ibid.

"between the size of . . .": "Notes on the Hessian Fly," June 1–15, 1792, *The Papers of Thomas Jefferson*, vol. 24, pp. 11–14. Founders Online, National Archives, founders.archives.gov/documents/Jefferson/01-24-02-0004.

"A 10. years abandonment . . .": letter from Jefferson to George Washington, May 14, 1794, *The Papers of George Washington*, Presidential Series, vol. 16, pp. 69–71. Founders Online, National Archives, founders.archives.gov/documents/Washington/05-16-02-0055.

"I return to farming . . .": letter from Jefferson to John Adams, April 25, 1794, *The Papers of Thomas Jefferson*, vol. 28, p. 57. Founders Online, National Archives, founders.archives.gov/documents/Jefferson/01-28-02-0055.

"more productive . . .": letter from Jefferson to Ferdinando Fairfax, April 25, 1794, *The Papers of Thomas Jefferson*, vol. 28, p. 58. Founders Online, National Archives, founders.archives.gov/documents/Jefferson/01-28-02-0056.

"The plough is to . . .": letter from Jefferson to Charles Willson Peale, April 17, 1813, *The Papers of Thomas Jefferson*, Retirement Series, vol. 6, pp. 68–70. Founders Online, National Archives, founders.archives.gov/documents/Jefferson/03-06-02-0069.

"the mould-board of . . .": letter from Jefferson to Sir John Sinclair, March 23, 1798, *The Papers of Thomas Jefferson*, vol. 30, pp. 197–209. Founders Online, National Archives, founders.archives.gov/documents/Jefferson/01-30-02-0135.

"that it may be made . . .": letter from Jefferson to John Taylor, December 29, 1794, *The Papers of Thomas Jefferson*, vol. 28, pp. 230–234. Founders Online, National Archives, founders.archives.gov/documents/Jefferson/01-28-02-0172.

"a rising nation . . .": Jefferson, "First Inaugural Address," in *Writings*, p. 492.

"The fertility of the country . . .": Jefferson, "Third Annual Message," in *Writings*, p. 512.

"explore the Missouri . . .": letter from Jefferson to Meriwether Lewis, June 20, 1803, Instructions. Library of Congress, The Thomas Jefferson Papers, Series 1, General Correspondence, 1651–1827, memory.loc.gov/cgi-bin/query/r?ammem/mtj:@field(DOCID+@lit(je00048)).

"I am constantly . . .": letter from Jefferson to Etienne Lemaire, April 25, 1809, *The Papers of Thomas Jefferson*, Retirement Series, vol. 1, pp. 161–162. Founders Online, National Archives, founders.archives.gov/documents/Jefferson/03-01-02-0133.

"The field of knolege . . .": letter from Jefferson to Henry Dearborn, June 22, 1807, Papers of Thomas Jefferson, Founders Early Access, Documents July 1804–March 3, 1809. University of Virginia Press, rotunda.upress.virginia.edu/founders/default.xqy?keys=FOEA-print-04-01-02-5793.

"I am closing the last scenes . . .": letter from Jefferson to Judge Augustus B. Woodward, April 3, 1825, *The Papers of Thomas Jefferson*, Retirement Series. Founders Online, National Archives, founders.archives.gov/documents/Jefferson/98-01-02-5105.

"academical village"; letter from Jefferson to Wilson C. Nicholas, April 2, 1816, in *The Writings of Thomas Jefferson* (ed. by Lipscomb and Bergh), vol. 14, p. 453.

"Planting a new world . . .": letter from Jefferson to John Page, March 18, 1803, American Antiquarian Society, Thomas Jefferson Papers, 1787–1825, Mss. Misc. Boxes J.

"When I first entered . . .": letter from Jefferson to Joseph Fay, March 18, 1793, *The Papers of Thomas Jefferson*, vol. 25, p. 402. Founders Online, National Archives, founders.archives.gov/documents/Jefferson/01-25-02-0364.

"They admit me a friend . . .": letter from Jefferson to William Jackson, February 18, 1801, *The Papers of Thomas Jefferson*, vol. 33, p. 14. Founders Online, National Archives, founders.archives.gov/documents/Jefferson/01-33-02-0010.

"in botany and in zoology . . .": Benjamin Smith Barton, quoted in *Twinleaf* newsletter by Lucia Stanton, 1992, monticello.org/site/house-and-gardens/twinleaf.

"Scheme for a System of Agricultural Societies": in *Writings of Thomas Jefferson* (ed. by Washington), vol. 9. p. 480.

"extensive and fertile Country": letter from Jefferson to George Rogers Clark, December 25, 1780, *The Papers of Thomas Jefferson*, vol. 4, pp. 233–238. Founders Online, National Archives, founders.archives.gov/documents/Jefferson/01-04-02-0295.

Text copyright © 2015 by Peggy Thomas
Illustrations copyright © 2015 by Stacy Innerst
All rights reserved

For information about permission to reproduce selections from this book, please contact permissions@highlights.com.

Calkins Creek
An Imprint of Highlights
815 Church Street
Honesdale, Pennsylvania 18431
Printed in China

ISBN: 978-1-62091-628-5
Library of Congress Control Number: 2014958527

First edition

10 9 8 7 6 5 4 3 2 1

Designed by Barbara Grzeslo
Production by Sue Cole
Text set in Cochin
About the illustrations and hand lettering: The illustrations were done in gouache on paper. I also incorporated scanned papers and textiles and, like Thomas Jefferson, I used a quill to write his words.
—*SI*

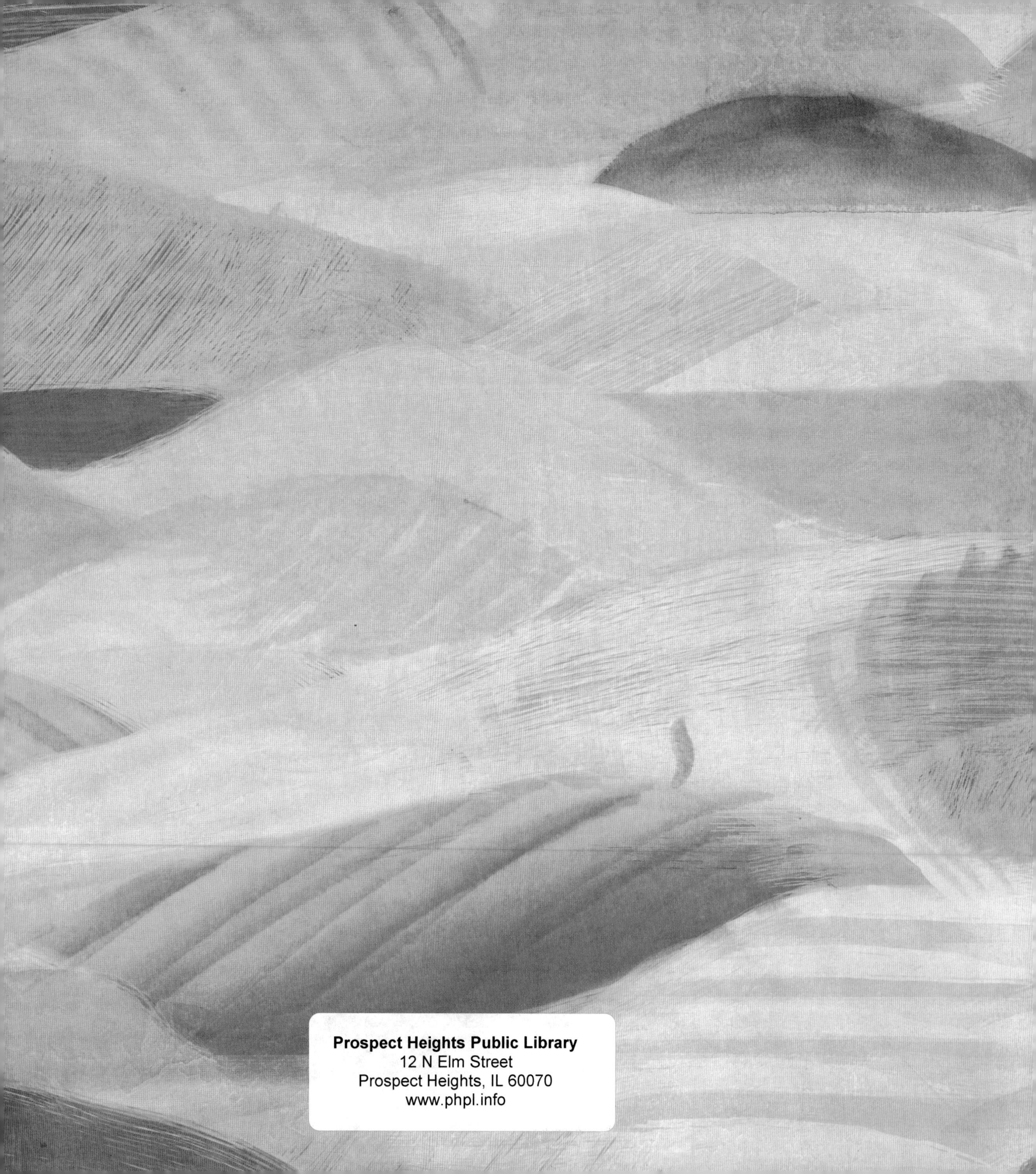